Wicked GERMAN

BY HOWARD TOMB
Illustrations by Jared Lee

WORKMAN PUBLISHING • NEW YORK

ACKNOWLEDGMENTS

Many thanks to Ulrike Dorda for her translation and Sally Kovalchick and Carbery O'Brien for their skill and patience.

Library of Congress Cataloging-in-Publication Data
Tomb, Howard
Wicked German for the traveler / by Howard Tomb.
p. cm.
ISBN 1-56305-294-6 (pbk.)
1. German language—Conversation and phrase books—Humor. 2. Voyages and travels—Humor.
3. Germany—Guidebooks—Humor. I. Title.
PN6231.G42T66   1992
438.3′421′0207—dc20 92-50289 CIP

Workman books are available at special discounts when purchased in bulk for premiums and sales promotions as well as for fund-raising or educational use. Special editions or book excerpts can also be created to specification.
For details, contact the Special Sales director at the address below.

Workman Publishing Company
708 Broadway
New York, NY 10003

Manufactured in the United States of America
First Printing October 1992

10 9

CONTENTS

WELCOME TO GERMANY

ACCOMMODATION, FOOD AND DRINK AND DRINK

DAILY LIFE

GETTING AROUND

GET A GRIP ON GERMAN

The German and English languages have intermingled over the centuries, thanks to the congress of monarchs, vast German immigration and informative T.V. programs such as *Hogan's Heroes.*

The two languages are so similar that we can grasp many German phrases upon first hearing. Some, including *ersatz, kitsch* and *dreck,* have entered English in their original form.

Others are understandable despite spelling differences, such as *bringen* (bring), *Blume* (flower), *dumm* (intellectually challenged), and *Pudel* (poodle).

Travelers who learn a few words will be able to decipher dozens of common phrases. Once you know that *aus* means "out," for example, you can guess the meaning of *aushängen, ausbomben* and *ausflippen.**

But sensing what Germans mean is not enough; you must be ready to counter with sharp ripostes. These issue from the back of the throat between the points of gargle and gag. A loud, stern voice and a couple of tablespoons of saliva add emphasis.

Armed with these phrases, a rigid attitude and a haughty bearing, you will win the battles fought by travelers since Romans first crossed the Alps. Or at least vent your frustrations.

Viel Glück

* hang out, bomb out, flip out

PRONUNCIATION GUIDE

German pronunciation is every bit as precise as a Hasselblad camera or a Glock automatic pistol. Even if our mouths were made of the finest Ruhr Valley steel, we foreigners could never achieve perfect pronunciation. Bettering our fellow tourists' pronunciation is easy, however, if we follow these simple rules.

Vowel sounds are absolutely distinct: *a* = "ah," *e* = "ay," *i* = "ee," *o* = "oh," *u* = "oo" and *ü* = "euyuue." The *ü* is an "eee" sound made with the lips protruding as if to suck foam from an overflowing stein.

Early Germans, known as Neanderthals, discovered two special "ch" sounds. The hard "ch" is formed after the vowels a, o, u, and au, furball-like at the back of the throat. This hard "ch" does not exist in English but has survived in Hebrew.

The soft "ch," even more difficult, hisses further forward in the mouth and is formed after the vowels e, i, ä, ü, ie, ei, äu, eu. As the fat part of the tongue nears the palate, the hissing begins.

Make these sounds each day for exactly two hours before breakfast and exactly two hours after dinner. As your back begins to straighten and your facial muscles freeze up, you'll begin to look and feel more German. You've captured the essence of the Teutonic spirit, and doing that is the secret to learning any language.

TALK IN THE PROVINCES

German scholars believe that spoken German includes dialects from three basic categories: High, Low, and *Ausländisch.*

Dutch and Flemish are said to be forms of Low German. Yiddish derives from High German while French, Italian, Polish, Russian and Greek are all dialects from the third category: *Ausländisch.* Apparently the German "Uberlanguage" was spread across the continent by roving tribes of stern German schoolteachers.

The university, or High, German used in this book makes it useful all over Germany, Austria and Switzerland, allowing readers to subdue wrathful Goths wherever they are found.

LINGUISTIC DISCLAIMER AND EXCULPATORY PROTESTATION

The author and his translators, agents, publisher, editors, attorneys, heirs, personal friends and armed bodyguards hereby throttle, pummel and utterly humiliate any claim, tort or tart arising from the use or misuse of words, phrases, concepts or attitudes contained herein.

ACCOMMODATION, FOOD AND DRINK 🍺

HOTEL EXISTENCE

Almost all Germans—including hotel staff—share an interest in philosophy. Sprinkling your complaints with quotes from native thinkers will enhance your prestige around the *Gasthaus* much more than any threat or gold card possibly could.

IMMANUEL KANT (1724–1804)		
Time and space exist only in our minds.	*Zeit und Raum existieren nur in unseren Köpfen.*	*TSEIT oont ROWM ai-xis-TEE-ren noor in OON-zay-ren KUHP-fen.*
Where the hell is room service?	*Wo zum Teufel bleibt der Zimmerservice?*	*VOH tsoom TOY-fel bleibt dair TSIM-mair-SURH-vees?*

ARTHUR SCHOPENHAUER (1788–1860)		
No matter how deeply we investigate, we can never reach anything except images and names.	*Wie immer man auch forschen mag: so gewinnt man nichts als Bilder und Namen.*	*Vee EEM-mair mahn owkh FOHR-shen makh: zoh gay-VEENNT mahn NEEKHTS ahls BEEL-dair oont NAH-men.*
Although I do smell a foul odor in the bathroom area.	*Obwohl ich einen faulen Geruch um das Badezimmer herum rieche.*	*Ohp-vohl eekh EI-nen FOW-len gay-ROOKH oom dahs BAH-deh-TSIM-mer hair-OOM REE-kheh.*

FRIEDRICH NIETZSCHE (1844–1900)

I have plumbed the depths in the soul of the highest man.	*Ich habe die Tiefen in der Seele des höchsten Menschen ergründet.*	*Eekh HAH-beh dee TEE-fen in dair ZAY-leh dess HUHKH-sten MEN-shen air-GREWN-deht.*
Now fetch me some sedatives.	*Nun holen Sie mir ein Beruhigungsmittel.*	*Noon HOH-len zee meer ein bay-ROO-ee-goon(g)z MEET-tel.*

GOTTFRIED WILHELM LEIBNIZ (1646-1716)

There is no chaos or confusion.	*Es gibt kein Chaos, keine Verwirrung.*	*Ess geebt kein KAH-ohs, KEI-neh fair-VEER-roon(g).*
It only looks that way to the maid.	*Der Magd ersheint es nur so.*	*Dair MAHKT air-SHEINT ess noor ZOH.*

ACCOMMODATION, FOOD AND DRINK 🍺

HISTORY IN BEER

Germans make many things well, and beer is among their greatest achievements. Its exact origins have been lost among thousands of groggy mornings and sledgehammer headaches, but this is what scholars now believe about beer's history.

---

c. 20,000 B.C. Og of Url eats a handful of yeast with  his gruel and water. He is hailed as the Father of Beer and Life of the Party at his funeral the next day.

---

c. 11,000 B.C. Herman of Villendorf drinks 12 steins of lager in 1.79 seconds, breaking the world record. His subsequent belch also sets a record, killing 28.

---

c. 6000 B.C. Henrik the Effete, the first beer connoisseur, invents the sip. He is banished to France.

---

c. 1516 B.C. The German Purity Law is written to protect the quality of beer. Anyone caught drinking Coors is spanked to death by a 300-pound barmaid.

500 A.D. Huns descend on Germany looking for riches, virgins, pretzels and a genuine fire-brewed beer with no aftertaste.

501–1870 Hun celebration.

1871 Otto von Bismarck settles Germany's major dispute and unites the nation with his decree on Dinkel Acker Light: Tastes great *and* less filling.

1961 Berlin Wall erected. East German government bans every brand of beer except Harnburgh. The party appears to be over.

1990 East Germans, hearing rumors about the classic taste of ice-cold Spaten, knock down the Berlin Wall, party nonstop and run up a six-billion-dollar bar tab.

ACCOMMODATION, FOOD AND DRINK 🍺

BEER-HALL SMALL TALK

Biergärten or *Hofbräuhäuser* (beer halls) can be as big and noisy as gyms. When strangers sit down and attempt to engage you in conversation use one or more of these all-purpose rejoinders.

Cheers/health/ Fatherland!	*Prost/Gesundheit/ Vaterland!*	*Prohst/Ge-ZOONT-height/ FAH-tair-lahnd!*
Here's mud/spit in your eye!	*Da ist Dreck/Spucke in Ihrem Auge!*	*Dah isst DRAIK/ SHPOOK-uh een EE-ren OW-geh!*
I agree completely!	*Ganz meine Meinung!*	*GAHNTS mei-neh MEI-noong!*
But that happens to be my wife/husband!	*Aber das ist nur meine Frau/mein Mann!*	*AH-bair DAHS ist noor mei-neh FROW/mein MAHN!*
Now you've crossed the line, you bag of schnitzel!	*Nun haben Sie aber die Grenze überschritten, Sie Schnitzelrancher!*	*Noon HAH-ben zee AH-bair dee GREN-tseh EW-bair-SHRIT-ten, zee SHNIT-sel-RAN-chur!*
Goodnight, my friend! Nice knowing you!	*Gute Nacht, mein Freund! War nett, Sie kennengelernt zu haben!*	*Goo-teh NAHKHT, mein froynt! Vahr net, zee KEN-nen-ge-lairnt tsoo HAH-ben!*

BEER CONNOISSEURSHIP

Beer is to Germans what wine is to the French. Impress your hosts by speaking knowingly about beer in a loud, authoritative voice.

This Malz has a strong oak flavor with a faint almond backwash.	*Dieses Malzbier hat einen starken Eichengeschmack und beim Aufstoßen schmeckt es leicht nach Mandeln.*	*DEE-zess MAHLTS-beer haht ein-en SHTAHR-ken EI-khen-ge-SHMAHK oont beim OWF-shtohs-sen shmehkt ess leikht nahkh MAHN-deln.*

The Hefe-Weizen has big feet and a small head.	*Weizenbier hat große Füße und einen kleinen Kopf.*	*VEI-tsayn-beer haht GROH-seh FEW-seh oont ei-nen KLEI-nen KOHPF.*
You can taste eggs beneath the vigorous schnauzer.	*Sie können Eier unter diesem vitalen Schnauzer schmecken.*	*Zee kuhn-nen EI-er oon-tair dee-zehm vee-TAHL-en SHNOW-tser shmek-ken.*

ACCOMMODATION, FOOD AND DRINK

The tanned, curvaceous Rauchbier displays a fine set of bubbles.	*Das gebräunte, kurvenreiche Rauchbier zeigt einen feinen Satz von Blasen.*	*Dahs geh-BROIN-teh, KOOR-vehn-rei-kheh ROWKH-beer tseikt ei-nen FEI-nen ZAHTS fohn BLAH-zehn.*

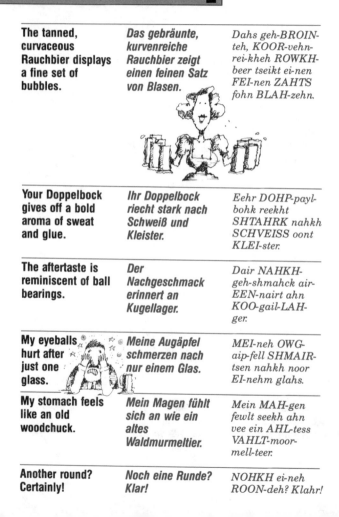

Your Doppelbock gives off a bold aroma of sweat and glue.	*Ihr Doppelbock riecht stark nach Schweiß und Kleister.*	*Eehr DOHP-payl-bohk reekht SHTAHRK nahkh SCHVEISS oont KLEI-ster.*
The aftertaste is reminiscent of ball bearings.	*Der Nachgeschmack erinnert an Kugellager.*	*Dair NAHKH-geh-shmahck air-EEN-nairt ahn KOO-gail-LAH-ger.*
My eyeballs hurt after just one glass.	*Meine Augäpfel schmerzen nach nur einem Glas.*	*MEI-neh OWG-aip-fell SHMAIR-tsen nahkh noor EI-nehm glahs.*
My stomach feels like an old woodchuck.	*Mein Magen fühlt sich an wie ein altes Waldmurmeltier.*	*Mein MAH-gen fewlt seekh ahn vee ein AHL-tess VAHLT-moor-mell-teer.*
Another round? Certainly!	*Noch eine Runde? Klar!*	*NOHKH ei-neh ROON-deh? Klahr!*

A VISIT TO BLITZ

Just as Eskimos are said to have a hundred words for snow, Germans have a vast vocabulary to describe different depths of inebriation. Six representative categories are included here so that you may better explain someone's condition to the authorities.

Looking-deep-into-one's-stein	*Zu tief ins Glas gucken*	*Tsoo TEEF innz GLAHS gook-ken*
Becoming-the-monkey	*Der hat einen Affen*	*Dair haht EI-nen AHF-fen*
Touching-the-barmaid-without-the-permission	*Der Bardame ohne Erlaubnis in den Hintern Kneifen.*	*Dair BAHR-dah-meh OH-neh air-LOWP-niss in dain HEEN-tairn KNEI-fen.*
Springing-the-leaking	*Sich in die Hosen machen*	*Seekh in dee HOH-zeh MAH-khayn*
Sucking-the-gravel-in-the-parking-lot	*Auf dem Parkplatz in den Kies beißen*	*Owf daim PAHRK-plahts in dain KEES BEI-sen*
Dead-as-the-old-Elvishoffer	*Tot wie der alte Elvishoffer*	*Toht vee dair ahl-teh EL-VEES-hoh-fair*

YOUR OKTOBERFEST EMERGENCY

Oktoberfest is Munich's annual carnival of intoxication. Good manners require that you consume alcohol as if it were air. Memorize these emergency phrases.

Hey, guys. Are you able to stand up?	*Hallo Sie da. Können Sie gerade stehen?*	*Hal-loh SEE dah. KUHN-nen zee geh-RAH-deh SHTAY-en?*
Would you help me carry my friend?	*Würden Sie mir meinen Freund tragen helfen?*	*VYER-den zee meer mei-nen FROYNT TRAH-gen HELL-fen?*
Thanks, but I don't think pork/pretzels/hazelnut schnapps can help him now.	*Danke, aber Schweinefleisch/ Bretzeln/ Haselnußschnaps wird ihm jetzt wohl nicht helfen.*	*DAHN-keh, ah-bair SHVEI-neh-fleish/ BRAY-tseln/ HAH-zail-nooss-schnahps veert eem yetst vohl NEEKHT HELL-fen.*
I think he's coming to.	*Ich glaube, er kommt wieder zu sich.*	*EEKH GLOW-beh, air KOHMMT vee-dair tsoo zeekh.*
Hey! It sounds like he's learned to speak German!	*Hey! Es hört sich so an, als hätte er Deutsch gelernt!*	*Hay! Ess HUHRT seekh zoh AHN, ahls HEH-teh air DOYCH geh-LAIRNT!*

DOWN AND DIRTY IN THE *RATSKELLER*

Sigmund Freud was one of history's most fearless explorers—he entered the filthy, twisted minds of the Victorian middle class. Their descendants can be found in the local *Ratskeller,* the restaurant lying beneath every *Rathaus* (town hall). Try a little Freudian lip with your waiter or waitress.

I ordered bratwurst but you brought me bloodwurst.	*Ich habe Bratwurst bestellt und dennoch haben Sie mir Blutwurst gebracht.*	*Eekh HAH-beh BRAHT-voorst be-SHTAYLT oont DEN-nohkh HAH-ben zee meer BLOOT-voorst geh-BRAHKHT.*
Could it be you have fallen in love with me?	*Haben Sie sich etwa in mich verliebt?*	*HAH-ben zee SEEKH et-vah in meekh vair-LEEPT?*

ACCOMMODATION, FOOD AND DRINK

You have an unconscious wish that I eat your sauerkraut.	*Sie wünschen im Unterbewußten, daß ich Ihr Sauerkraut esse.*	*Zee VEWN-shen im OON-tair-beh-VOOSS-ten, dahss eekh eer ZOW-air-krowt ess-eh.*
Yet that is clearly a fantasy.	*Aber das ist offensichtlich eine Phantasie.*	*Ah-bair dahs isst OFF-fen-SEEKHT-leekh ei-neh FAHN-tah-ZEE.*
Naturally, I would enjoy a piece of your strudel.	*Natürlich hätte ich gerne ein Stück von Ihrem Strudel.*	*Nah-TEWR-leekh heh-teh eekh GAIR-neh ein SHTEWK fohn EE-rem SHTROO-dell.*
I suggest you stop in for a lie on my couch.	*Ich würde vorschlagen, Sie kommen vorbei und legen sich eine Weile auf meine Couch.*	*Eekh vewr-deh FOR-shlah-gen, zee KOHM-men for-BEI oont LAY-gen seekh ei-neh VEI-leh owf MEI-neh KOWCH.*

HOW TO BECOME A GERMAN DISHWASHER

The many *Neiberlunders* (restaurateurs) who don't accept credit cards will be upset after you consume barrels of food and alcohol and can't pay in cash. The Wicked Traveler negotiates with aplomb, however, even when surrounded by cleaver-wielding waiters.

You don't accept credit cards!?	*Sie akzeptieren keine Kreditkarten!?*	*Zee ahk-tsep-TEE-ren KEI-neh KRAY-deet-KAR-ten!?*
The bill seems remarkably high for noodles/potatoes/cabbage/organ meats.	*Diese Rechnung ist ganz schön hoch für Nudeln/Kartoffeln/Kohl/Innereien.*	*Dee-zeh REKH-noon(g) isst gahnz shern HOHKH fewr NOO-deln/Kahr-TOFF-eln/KOHL/ EEN-nair-EI-en.*
Hmm. I haven't enough marks to pay the bill.	*Hmm. Ich habe nicht genug Mark, um die Rechnung zu bezahlen.*	*Hmm. Eekh hah-beh neekht ge-nookh MAHRK, oom dee RAYKH-noong tsoo bay-TSAH-len.*
I do have some dollar-denominated traveler's checks.	*Ich habe einige Dollar-Reiseschecks.*	*Eekh hah-beh ei-nee-geh DOH-lahr-REI-zeh-shecks.*

ACCOMMODATION, FOOD AND DRINK 🍺

Watch it, fella. You're talking about my national currency.	*Vorsicht, mein Freund. Sie reden über meine Landeswährung.*	*FOR-seekht, mein FROYNT. Zee RAY-den ew-bair mei-neh LAHN-dess-VAIR-oon(g).*
You can check today's newspaper for the exchange rate.	*Sie können den Wechselkurs in der heutigen Zeitung nachsehen.*	*Zee kuhn-nen dain VECK-sel-koors in dair HOY-tee-gen TSEI-toon(g) NAHKH-zay-en.*
Or I'll return the meal to you.	*Oder Sie kriegen das Essen zurück.*	*OH-dair zee KREE-gen dahs ESS-en tsoo-REWK.*
With my compliments to the chef.	*Mit meinen Komplimenten an den Koch.*	*Mit MEI-nen kohm-plee-MEN-ten ahn dain KOHK.*

THE COST OF MONEY

German banks are surrounded by some of the world's thickest bureaucracy. Efforts to get around it will only make matters worse.

I'd like to cash this traveler's check.	*Ich möchte diesen Reisescheck eintauschen.*	*Eekh MUHKH-teh DEE-zen REI-zeh-sheck EIN-tow-shen.*
My credit cards, passport, driver's license and a signed photograph of Karl Malden?	*Meine Kreditkarten, mein Paß, mein Führerschein und ein Foto mit dem Autogramm von Karl Malden?*	*Mei-neh KRAY-dit-KAHR-ten, mein PAHSS, mein FEWR-rair-shein oont ein FOH-toh mit daim OW-toh-GRAHM fohn KAHRL MALL-den?*
No trouble—I have them right here.	*Kein Problem—ich habe das alles hier.*	*Kein proh-BLAIM-eekh hah-beh dahs ahl-less HEER.*
Would you also like to see my birthmark?	*Möchten Sie mein Muttermal sehen?*	*MUHKH-ten zee mein MOOT-tair-mahl Zay-en?*
It looks exactly like Munch's *The Scream*.	*Er sieht genau wie Munchs Der Schrei aus.*	*Air zeet gen-NOW vee MUHNKHS dair SCHREI ows.*

ABSOLUTE WURSTS

A trip to the
Metzger (butcher)
can be confusing;
the ever-inventive
Germans eat more
than a thousand var-
ieties of sausage. A few simple
questions can help you identify
things you wouldn't want to put in your mouth.

Which animal was this?	*Was für ein Tier war das?*	*VAHS fewr ein TEER vahr dahs?*
Which part?	*Welcher Teil?*	*Vell-khair TEIL?*
Please just point to the place on your own body.	*Bitte zeigen Sie mir die Stelle an Ihrem Körper.*	*BIT-teh TSEI-gen zee meer dee SHTEL-leh ahn EER-em KER-per.*
Hmm. That doesn't look very tasty/ healthful.	*Hmm. Das sieht mir nicht beson- ders schmackhaft/ gesund aus.*	*Hmm. Dahs zeet meer NEEKHT beh-ZOHN-dairz SHMAHK-hahft/ geh-ZUNT ows.*
Did I mention that I've decided to become a vegetarian?	*Habe ich erwähnt, daß ich mich entschlossen habe, Vegetarier zu werden?*	*Hah-be eekh air-VAINT, dahss eekh meekh ent-SHLOHS-sen hah-beh, VEH-geh-tair-EER tsoo VAIR-den?*

THE WORST OF THE WURSTS

This guide is provided for those who want to identify menu items and avoid trying anything new.

CHARMING GERMAN NAME	ACTUAL STUFFING
Aalgeleewurst*	jellied eels
Cervelatwurst*	scent organs
Gänseleberwurst*	swollen goose livers
Geflügelwurst*	things with wings
Lammzungenwurst*	tongues of lambs
Leberkäswurst*	clotted liver paste
Münchner Weisswurst*	brains of calves
Milzwurst*	slippery spleen meats
Rauhwurst*	assorted sardine parts
Schweineherzwurst*	well-marbled pig hearts
Wurstwurst*	defective wurst

*Indicates Non-Kosher

DAILY LIFE 🍺

PHONE CALL FOR MR. KAFKA

In formerly Communist areas, the German phone system still runs largely on Stalinist technology and attitudes. Operators continue to respond better to orders than to requests.

Operator, what is the area code for Munich?	*Was ist die Vorwahl für München?*	*VAHS isst dee FOR-vahl fewr MEWN-khen?*
Ha! It is nonsense to say that area codes are classified.	*So ein Quatsch zu sagen, daß Vorwahlnummern Geheimsache sind.*	*ZOH ein KVAHTCH tsoo ZAH-gen, dahss FOR-vahl-NOOM-mairn geh-HEIM-sah-khe zint.*
Don't you know who I am?	*Sie wissen wohl nicht, wer ich bin?*	*Zee VISS-en vohl neekht, VAIR eekh bin?*
I happen to have your file right here.	*Ich habe zufällig Ihre Akte gerade hier.*	*Eekh hah-beh TSOO-fay-leekh EE-reh AHK-teh geh-RAH-deh heer.*
I'll have your hazelnuts in a vise, my friend.	*Ich werde Ihre Brötchen unter Beschuß nehmen, meine Gute.*	*Eekh VAIR-deh EE-reh BREWT-khen oon-tair beh-SHOOSS NAY-men, mei-neh GOO-teh.*

You'll wish you'd been born in Bulgaria.	*Sie werden sich wünschen, in Bulgarien geboren worden zu sein.*	*Zee VAIR-den seekh VEWN-shen, in bool-GAHR-ee-en geh-BOH-ren vohr-den tsoo zein.*
Put me through to Munich immediately!	*Verbinden Sie mich auf der Stelle mit München!*	*Fair-BIN-den zee meekh OWF dair SHTEL-leh mit MEWN-khen!*

POST COMMUNIST

Formerly East German postal workers haven't broken the habit of reading other people's mail. To keep your correspondence private, use the following.

CODE WORD (ENGLISH)	ACTUAL MEANING	CODE WORD (GERMAN)
Gretel	having	Gretl
feels	a	fühlt sich
quite	good	ziemlich
ill	time	krank
and	wish	und
smells	you	riecht
worse	were	schlimmer
daily	here	von einem Tag zum anderen

SHOPPING FOR LAUGHS

If money and style mean nothing to you, you might enjoy shopping for clothes in Germany. Berlin has an especially bizarre variety of stores and fashions. Even if you can't afford to buy anything, you can have fun with sales help.

Hey! I've never seen a comedy clothing store before!	*Hallo! Ich habe nie zuvor einen Kleiderladen für Komödianten gesehen!*	*HAHL-loh! Eekh HAH-beh NEE tsoo-for ein-en KLEI-dair-LAH-den fewr koh-muh-dee-AHN-ten ge-ZAY-en!*
These lederhosen/jackets/ties are hilarious!	*Diese Hosen/Jacketts/Krawatten sind einfach um-werfend!*	*Dee-zeh HOH-zen/Jahk-KETS/Krah-VAHT-ten zint ein-fahkh OOM-vair-fent!*
Do you have anything out of the brown area of the spectrum?	*Haben Sie etwas außerhalb des braunen Farbspektrums?*	*Hah-bayn zee ET-vahs OW-zair-hahlp dess BROW-nen FAHRP-shpeck-troomz?*
What great loden coats/Tyrolean hats/mod shoes!	*Was für tolle Lodenmäntel Tirolerhüte/modische Schuhe!*	*Vahs fyoor TOHL-leh LOH-den-MEN-tell/tee-ROH-lair-hew-teh/moh-dish-eh SHOO-eh!*

So heavy/goofy/ German!	*So schwer/ vertrottelt/deutsch!*	*Zoh SHVAIR fair- TROHT-tellt DOYCH!*
I'll take them all!	*Ich nehme das alles!*	*Eekh NAY-meh dahs AHL-less!*
Charge my Barnum & Bailey account.	*Stellen Sie es meinem Konto bei Barnum & Bailey in Rechnung.*	*SHTEL-len zee ess MEI-nem KOHN-toh bei Barnum & Bailey in REKH-noon(g).*

DAILY LIFE 🏠

YOU AND THE SWISS ARMY KNIFE

When shopping for souvenirs, resist salespeople's attempts to sell you a model with more bells and whistles than you really need. German products are expensive enough already.

Hello, I'd like to buy a camera/pair of binoculars/fondue set.	*Hallo, ich hätte gerne eine Kamera/Ferngläser/Fonduegeschirr.*	*HAHL-loh, eekh heht-teh gair-neh ei-neh KAH-meh-rah/FAIRN-glay-zer/fohn-DEW-geh-SHEER.*
Do you have one without a belt punch/electronic brain?	*Haben Sie ein Gerät ohne Lochzange/Elektrogehirn?*	*Hah-ben Zee ein geh-RAIT OH-neh LOHKH-tsahng-eh/ay-LEKH-troh-geh-heern?*
It is superior, I'm sure.	*Ich bin sicher, es ist von auserlesener Qualität.*	*Eekh bin SEEKH-er, ess ist fohn OWZ-air-LAY-zen-er kvah-lee-TAIT.*
But I don't need 400 horsepower.	*Aber ich brauche keine 400 PS.*	*AH-bair eekh BROW-kheh kei-neh FEER-hoon-dairt PS.*
I think I'll just take this commemorative key chain.	*Ich denke, ich nehme nur diesen Schlüsselbund als Andenken.*	*Eekh DINK-eh, eekh NAY-meh NOOR DEE-zen SHLUHS-sell-boont ahls AHN-dink-en.*

SURVIVING THE AUTOBAHN

No trip to Germany would be complete without the testosterone charge of competitive driving in a borrowed car. With enough brow beating, most rental agents will supply you with a car that burns rubber in every gear. Don't settle for less.

I requested an automobile, not a golf cart.	*Ich habe ein Auto bestellt und nicht ein Golfmobil.*	*Eekh HAH-beh ein OW-toh beh-SHTELLT oont neekht ein GOHLF-moh-beel.*
This child's toy struggles to reach 225 kilometers.	*Dieses Kinderspielzeug quält sich ab, 225 Kilometer zu erreichen.*	*Dee-zess KIN-dair-shpeel-tsoyk KVAILT seekh AHP, TSVEI-hoon-dairt-FUHNF-oont-TSVAHN-tseekh KEE-loh-may-ter tsoo air-REI-khen.*
I refuse to be humiliated by you or by other drivers.	*Ich weigere mich, von Ihnen oder anderen Fahrern beleidigt zu werden.*	*Eekh VEI-gair-eh meekh, fohn EE-nen oh-dair AHN-dair-en FAHR-airn beh-LEI-dikt tsoo VAIR-den.*
Give me twelve cylinders or a full refund.	*Geben Sie mir zwölf Zylinder oder mein Geld zurück.*	*GAY-ben zee meer ZVUHLF TSEE-len-der oh-der mein GELT tsoo-RUHK.*

ROAD CURSES AND FINES

Slandering the mean-spirited German motorist is richly satisfying even though Germans actually fine motorists who shout specific curses while driving. Use this price list to decide what you can afford.

SLUR	TRANSLATION	FINE
Damischer Bulle *DAH-mee-shair-BOOL-leh*	stupid bull	$2,760
Raubritter *ROWB-reet-tair*	robber baron	$2,080
Depp *Depp*	idiot	$1,175
Stinkstiefel *SHTINK-shtee-fell*	smelly boot	$729
Knolle *KNOHL-leh*	tuber	$425
Rchtlfrtzlkraut	(unintelligible)	$100
Wichtigtuer *VEEKH-teekh-too-air*	poo-poo head	2 for 99¢

ROAD SIGNS

Before getting behind the wheel in Germany, be sure to memorize the country's unique road signs.

NO SENSE OF HUMOR
NEXT 1200 KM

BEER HALL AREA
PREPARE STEINS

STRAIGHTAWAY NEXT 1.6 KM
STOMP DAS PEDAL TO DER METAL

WATCH FOR
FALLING DOLLAR

SLOW:
ELF CROSSING

GETTING AROUND 🚗

THE POLICEMAN'S BEAT

Polizei (police officers) are officious and notoriously unhelpful to foreigners. Luckily, they can be paralyzed by anyone who dares to defy them.

Officer, please direct me to Wartburg?	*Wachtmeister, können Sie mir sagen, wie ich zur Wartburg komme?*	*VAHKHT-mei-stair, KUHN-nen zee meer ZAH-gen, vee EEKH tsoor VAHRT-boorg kohm-meh?*
You want to see my passport?	*Sie wollen meinen Paß sehen?*	*Zee VOHL-len mei-nen PAHSS ZAY-en?*
Don't be an idiot.	*Seien Sie kein Idiot.*	*ZEI-en zee KEIN ee-dee-OHT.*
I've got a castle tour in 15 minutes.	*Ich habe in 15 Minuten eine Führung durch die Burg.*	*Eekh HAH-beh in FUHNF-tsain mee-NOO-ten ei-neh FEW-roon(g) doorkh dee BOORG.*
Maybe you didn't hear me the first time, brick wit.	*Vielleicht haben Sie mich beim erstenmal nicht gehört, Sie Hohlkopf.*	*Feel-LEIKHT hah-ben zee meekh beim AIR-sten-mahl neekht geh-HUHRT, zee HOHL-kopf.*

Tell me where to find the castle or kiss my dirndl, dachshund breath.	*Sagen Sie mir, wo ich die Burg finde, oder küssen Sie mein Dirndl, Sie räudiger Dackel.*	*ZAH-gen zee MEER, VOH eekh die BOORG FIN-deh, oh-dair KUHS-sen zee mein DEERN-del, zee ROY-dih-gair DAHK-kel.*
Thank you for letting me ride in your squad car.	*Danke, daß Sie mich in Ihrem Streifenwagen mitnehmen.*	*DAHN-keh, dahss zee meekh in EE-rem SHTREI-fen-VAH-gen MIT-nay-men.*
Now I am sure to reach the castle on time.	*Nun bin ich sicher, daß ich die Burg rechtzeitig erreichen werde.*	*Noon bin eekh SIKH-er, dahss eekh dee BOORG REKHT-tsei-tikh air-REI-khen vair-deh.*

GETTING AROUND 🚗

SERVE AND PROTECT

German highway patrol officers are always on the lookout for weak, hesitant drivers who throw kinks into the blur of *Autobahn* traffic. Speaking their language is a sure way to avoid misunderstandings.

What seems to be the problem, officer?	*Was scheint das Problem zu sein, Herr Wachtmeister?*	*Vahs sheint dahs proh-BLAIM tsoo zein, hair VAHKHT-mei-stair?*
I had to ram him/her off the road, of course.	*Ich mußte ihn/sie natürlich von der Straße rammen.*	*Eekh MOOSS-teh een/zee nah-TEWR-leekh fohn dair SHTRAH-seh RAHM-men.*
He/she was driving dangerously slow in the fast lane.	*Er/Sie fuhr wirklich gefährlich langsam in der Überholspur.*	*AIR/ZEE foohr veerk-leekh gey-FAIR-leekh LAHN(G)-zahm in dair EW-bair-HOHL-shpoor.*
No more than 240 kilometers an hour!	*Nicht mehr als 240 Stundenkilometer!*	*NEEKHT mair ahls TSVAL-hoon-dairt-VEER-tseekh SHTOON-den-kee-loh-may-tir!*

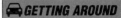

No, thank *you*, officer.	*Nein, vielen Dank, Herr Wachtmeister.*	*NINE, FEE-len DAHNK, hair VAHKHT-mei-stair.*
Keep up the good work!	*Machen Sie nur so weiter!*	*MAH-khen zee NOOR zoh VEI-tair!*

SOCIALISM THROUGH AUTOMOBILES

The achievements of East German socialism included boredom, dough-like complexions, air pollution you could eat with a spoon and the Trabant. Compare this car-like object to the pinnacle of capitalist West German automotive efforts.

	BMW 750i	TRABANT Tin Chipmunk
Power-Assisted Steering	✔	
Anti-Lock Brakes	✔	
Custom Fuel Injection	✔	
400 Horsepower	✔	
Coal-Powered		✔
Handy Pull-Starter		✔
Genuine Wood Gearbox		✔
Fits Easily in a Suitcase		✔

CONFESSIONS OF A SINNER

Germans love to follow rules and they want you to follow them, too. Jaywalking, for example, is likely to get you a stern lecture from a concerned citizen. Your counterattack should be merciless.

Ha! That was nothing.	*Ha! Das war nichts.*	*Hah! DAHS vahr NEEKHTS.*
Tuesday I threw a gum wrapper in the town square.	*Am Dienstag warf ich ein Kaugummipapier auf den Marktplatz.*	*Ahm DEENS-tahk VAHRF eekh ein KOW-goom-mee-pah-PEER owf dain MAHRKT-plahts.*
I unleashed my dog in the park!	*Ich habe meine Hundin im Park von der Leine gelassen!*	*Eekh HAH-beh mei-neh HUHNT im PAHRK fohn dair LEI-neh geh-LAHS-sen!*
He peed on a bush!	*Er hat auf einen Busch gepinkelt!*	*Air HAHT owf ei-nen BOOSH geh-PINK-elt!*
Tomorrow I will ride my bicycle on the sidewalk!	*Morgen werde ich mein Fahrrad auf dem Bürgersteig fahren!*	*MOHR-gen VAIR-deh eekh mein FAHR-rad owf daim BUHR-gair-shteik FAHR-ren!*
Yes! I am a devil/ anarchist/ American!	*Ja! Ich bin ein Teufel/Anarchist/ Amerikaner!*	*YAH! Eekh bin ein TOY-fel/ah-nar-KHEEST/ah-may-ree-KAH-nair!*

MID-MORNING EXPRESS

In their rush for seats, some German men inexplicably hurl women and children aside. Freud felt that the seats themselves—made of unvarnished wood in his day—aroused the men sexually. Jung theorized that they regressed to their original ape-like selves and could not stand upright for more than a few moments. Regardless of the diagnosis, these creatures must be reminded of their duties.

Relax, there's no need to insult/shove/pummel anyone.	*Beruhigen Sie sich, sie brauchen keinen zu beleidigen/zu stoßen/mit Fäusten zu schlagen.*	*Beh-ROO-ee-gen ZEE zeekh. Zee BROW-khen KEI-nen tsoo beh-LEI-dee-gen/tsoo SHTOH-sen/mit FOY-sten tsoo SHLAH-gen.*
In fact, I would be willing to give you my seat.	*Ich bin in der Tat bereit, Ihnen meinen Platz zu überlassen.*	*EEKH bin in dair, TAHT beh-REIT, EE-nen MEI-nen PLAHTS tsoo ew-bair-LAHS-sen.*
But your butt is so big you'd need two.	*Aber Ihr Hintern ist so groß, daß Sie zwei brauchen.*	*AH-bair eer HEEN-tairn ist zoh GROHS, DAHSS zee TSVEI brow-khen.*
You belong in the baggage car.	*Sie gehören in den Gepäckwagen.*	*Zee geh-HUH-ren in dain geh-PECK-vah-gen.*

MYSTERY TRAIN

Train rides across the former frontier between East and West are agonizingly slow because the tracks have different gauges and riders must change trains. Trains in the East also run on a different timetable: the same one you'll find in the Twilight Zone. The conductor will be happy to clear things up for you.

Hello, Madam/ Mister/Comrade Conductor.	*Guten Tag, meine Dame/Herr/ Genosse Schaffner.*	*Goo-ten TAHK, mei-neh DAH-meh/hair/geh-NOHS-seh SHAHFF-nair.*
I'm glad to see you're preserving tradition.	*Ich freue mich zu sehen, daß Sie die Tradition aufrechterhalten.*	*Eekh FROY-eh meekh tsoo ZAY-en, dahss zee dee trah-dee-tsee-OHN OWF-rekht-air-HAHL-ten.*

I haven't seen stone wheels since I was a boy.	*Ich habe keine Steinräder gesehen, seit ich ein Junge war.*	*Eekh HAH-beh kei-neh SHTEIN-rai-dair geh-ZAY-en, zeit eekh ein YOON(G)eh vahr.*
But I am confused.	*Aber ich bin verwirrt.*	*Ah-bair EEKH bin fair-VEERT.*
Why are we stopped on this siding?	*Warum halten wir an diesem Rangiergleis an?*	*Vah-ROOM HAHL-ten veer ahn DEE-zem RAN-geer-gleiss ahn?*
I am growing thirsty/hungry/senile.	*Ich werde durstig/hungrig/senil.*	*Eekh VAIR-deh DOOR-shtikh/HOON(G)-reekh/zay-NEEL.*
Will we reach Berlin in this millennium?	*Werden wir Berlin in diesem Jahrtausend erreichen?*	*VAIR-den veer Bair-leen in DEE-zem yahr-TOW-zent air-REI-khen?*

GETTING AROUND 🚗

THE SPIRIT OF THE RED BARON

Efficient air travel depends on human organization and well-maintained machinery. Germans have extraordinary talents in these two areas, but perfection has yet to be achieved on Lufthansa, the German airline. Feel free to point out glitches to airline employees.

Steward(ess), according to my chronograph, we took off three minutes late.	*Steward(ess)! Nach meiner Uhr sind wir mit mehr als drei Minuten Verspätung abgeflogen.*	*Steward(ess)! Nakh MEI-nair OOR zint veer mit MAIR ahls DREI mee-NOO-ten fair-SHPAY-toon(g) AHP-geh-FLOW-gen.*
This is sparkling wine, not Champagne.	*Das is Sekt und nicht Champagner.*	*Dahs ist ZEKT oont NEEKHT shahm-PAHN-er.*
I'm going to complain to the Red Baron himself.	*Ich werde mich beim Roten Baron selbst beschweren.*	*Eekh VAIR-deh meekh beim ROH-ten bah-ROHN ZELPST beh-SHVAY-ren.*
What? He's dead?	*Was? Der ist tot?*	*VAHS? Dair ist TOHT?*
Then who the hell is flying the plane?	*Wer zum Teufel fliegt denn dann dieses Flugzeug?*	*VAIR tsoom TOY-fell fleekt den dahn DEE-zess FLOOK-tsoykh?*

THE FRONT LINES

Germans aren't in the habit of lining up and may try to sidle, waddle, elbow and shove past you. Most will show respect for the first-come-first-served rule, but only when gently reminded.

Yo. Dude.	*Ja. Sie.*	YAH. ZEE.
I was here before you came in.	*Ich war vor Ihnen hier.*	Eekh vahr FOHR EE-NEN heer.
And so were these customers, you swine person.	*Und so waren es diese Kunden, Sie Schweinehund.*	Oont ZOH vahr-en DEE-zeh KOON-den, zee SHWEIN-HOONT.
Don't tell us you're in a hurry to eat!	*Sagen Sie uns bloß nicht, Sie sind in Eile und müssen schnell was essen!*	ZAH-gen zee oons BLOHSS neekht, zee zint in EI-leh oont muhs-sen shnell vahs ESS-en!
Food is the last thing you need.	*Essen ist das letzte, was Sie brauchen.*	Ess-en isst dahs LETS-teh, vahs zee BROW-khayn.
Jog to the back of the line, buddy.	*Beweg dich an das Ende der Schlange, Kumpel.*	Beh-VAIG deekh ahn dahs EN-deh dair SHLAHNG-eh, KOOM-pell.

GRIMM TALES OF THE BLACK FOREST

Forests are central to many fables and the Black Forest is the granddaddy of them all. Amuse the locals by referring to fairy-tale adventures.

Say, aren't you a cruel dwarf/wolf in disguise?	*Sagen Sie, sind Sie nicht ein grausamer Zwerg/ verkleideter Wolf?*	*ZAH-gen zee, zint zee neekht ein GROW-zah-mair TSVAIRK/fair-KLEI-deh-ter VOHLF?*
We seek a golden ring/your head on a platter/a couple of cold beers.	*Wir suchen einen goldenen Ring/ Ihren Kopf auf einer Platte/zwei Glas kalten Bieres.*	*Veer ZOO-khen ei-nen GOLD-en-en RING/ee-ren KOHPF owf ei-nair PLAHT-teh/ tsvei glahs kahl-ten BEER-ess.*
What you just said is a riddle to me.	*Was Sie gerade sagten, ist mir ein Rätsel.*	*Vahs zee geh-RAH-deh zak-ten, ist meer ein RAIT-sell.*
Nevertheless, it sounded mighty rude.	*Trotzdem klang es unheimlich rüde.*	*TROHTS-daim klahng ess oon-HEIM-leekh REW-deh.*
Be gone, Evil One! Return to your filthy lair!	*Gehe dahin, Übler! Kehre zurück in deine dreckige Höhle!*	*GAY-eh dah-HIN, EW-blair! KAIR-eh tsoo-REWK in dei-neh DREK-ee-geh HUH-leh!*

IT'S ALL HAPPENING AT THE BERLIN ZOO

On a trip through Berlin, you're almost certain to visit the zoo. A combination transportation hub and menagerie, the zoo attracts many social and biological parasites. Your quick response to their presence will help you avoid infection.

Excuse me. Is this the zoo?	*Entschuldigen Sie. Ist das der Zoo?*	*Ent-SHOOL-dee-gen zee. Ist DAHS dair TSOH?*
No, I don't need a "date."	*Nein, ich brauche keine "Braut."*	*NINE, eekh BROW-kheh kei-neh "BROWT."*
Exactly what do you mean when you say "really good time"?	*Was meinen Sie genau, wenn Sie sagen: "wirklich gute Zeit"?*	*Vahs MEI-nen zee geh-NOW, venn zee ZAH-gen: "VEERK-leekh GOO-teh TSEIT"?*
Fifty marks? That's sickening.	*Fünfzig Mark? Da kann einem ja übel werden.*	*FUHNF-tseekh MAHRK? DAH kahn EI-nem yah EW-bell VAIR-den.*
Who let you out of your cage?	*Wer hat dich denn aus dem Käfig herausgelassen?*	*VAIR haht deekh denn ows daim KAY-feekh hair-OWS-geh-LAHS-sen?*

CASTLE CRITIQUE

No Bavarian holiday would be complete without a tour of at least one fairy-tale castle. If the owners are home, don't be intimidated by their titles or nobility— impress them with your intelligent questions and comments.

I understand this castle was built many years ago.	*Wie ich weiß, wurde dieses Schloß vor vielen Jahren gebaut.*	*Vee eekh VEISS, voor-deh dee-zess SHLOHSS for FEE-len YAH-ren geh-BOWT.*
Say, that is a handsome bannister.	*Das ist aber ein schönes Geländer.*	*Dahs ist ah-bair ein SHUH-ness geh-LEN-dair.*
Would you mind if my children took a slide or two?	*Hätten Sie was dagegen, wenn meine Kinder ein- oder zweimal runterrutschten?*	*HET-ten zee vahs dah-GAY-gen, venn MEI-neh KIN-dair EIN-oh-dair TSVEI-mahl ROON-tair-ROOCH-ten?*
So, how does Mrs. Ludwig keep up with the dusting?	*So, wie kommt Frau Ludwig mit dem Staubwischen nach?*	*ZOH, VEE kohmmt frow LOOD-weekh mit daim SHTOWB-vee-shen NAHKH?*

CRIB SHEET TO MAJOR MYTHS

Teutonic myths allow insight into the German character and the plots of endless, impenetrable operas, poems, novels and delusions. These "crib notes" will help you avoid the agony of studying the myths in their original forms.

THE NIBELUNGENLIED, A.K.A. THE RING

Herr Doktor Siegfried wields a sword made by Swiss elves. Herr Doktor Hagen kills him anyway and chucks the Rheingold, an absolutely corrupting treasure, into the Rhine. Most of the fish are killed.

HERR DOKTOR GEORG JOHANN FAUST

In *Faust: The Early Years,* the old doktor sells his soul to Mephistopheles for knowledge, eternal life, a young woman named Gretchen and a Biedermeier dinette set. Faust forgets to ask for Gretchen's immortality or medical insurance. Tragedy ensues.

THE SORROWS OF YOUNG WERTHER

Herr Doktoral Kandidate Werther, a brilliant but dreamy fellow, falls in love with Lotte, a girl with a slow wit and unusually large *Entchen*. He immediately loses her phone number and then can't remember her name. Distraught, he blows his brains out.

THE BADENEST BATHS IN GERMANY

Germany's mineral springs have been popular with rich rheumatic people since the Romans ruled. If you are rich and rheumatic—or just want to feel that way—be sure to visit a spa to get bathed, steamed and pummeled.

Don't allow a host or hostess to order you around. As a paying customer, you can say no to any part of the program.

I don't mind being stark naked in front of a group of stark naked strangers.	*Es macht mir nichts aus, vor einer Gruppe völlig nackter Fremder völlig nackt zu sein.*	*Ess MAHKHT meer NEEKHTS ows, fohr ei-nair GROOP-peh fuhl-leekh NAHK-tair FREM-dair fuhl-leekh NAHKT tsoo zein.*
As long as they are older and uglier than I.	*Solange sie älter und häßlicher sind als ich.*	*Zoh-LAHN(G)eh zee ELL-tair oont HESS-lee-khair zint ahls EEKH.*
Will people be offended if I avert my eyes?	*Werden die Leute sich beleidigt fühlen, wenn ich meine Augen abwende?*	*VAIR-den dee LOY-teh zeekh beh-LEI-deekht FUH-len, venn eekh MEI-neh OW-gen AHP-venn-deh?*

I will not allow that mud to touch my body.	*Ich werde nicht erlauben, das Schlamm meinen Körper zu berühren.*	*Eekh vair-deh neekht air-LOW-ben, das SHLAHM mei-nen KUHR-per tsoo beh-RUH-ren.*
I don't care about the curative powers—it's disgusting.	*Seine heilenden Kräfte sind mir wurscht; er ist ekelerregend.*	*ZEI-neh HEI-len-den KREHF-teh zint meer VOORSHT; air ist AY-kell-RAY-gent.*
By the way, how ill are the other bathers?	*Übrigens, wie krank sind die anderen Badenden?*	*EW-bree-genz, vee KRAHNK zint dee AHN-dair-en BAH-den-den?*
Can you tell me which ones are contagious?	*Können Sie mir sagen, wer von Ihnen ansteckende Krankheiten hat?*	*KUHN-nen zee meer ZAH-gen, VAIR fohn ee-nen AHN-shtek-ken-deh KRAHNK-hei-ten HAHT?*

THE PRETTY GOOD OUTDOORS

Germans love the wilderness and have been improving it since about 4000 B.C. Nothing upsets them more than criticism of their landscape, no matter how denuded it has become due to industrial development and acid rain. Comment only on the good things about the forests.

Your rugged mountains take my breath away.	*Ihre zerklüfteten Berge sind atemberaubend.*	*EE-reh tsair-KLUHF-teh-ten BAIR-geh zint AH-tem-beh-ROW-bent.*
Or perhaps it is the lack of oxygen.	*Oder vielleicht ist es der Mangel an Sauerstoff.*	*Oh-dair feel LEIKHT ist ess dair MAHN-gell ahn ZOW-air-shtohff.*
I sighted several trees this morning.	*Heute morgen erspähte ich mehrere Bäume.*	*HOY-teh MOHR-gen air-SHPAY-teh eekh MAIR-eh-reh BOY-meh.*
Also a squirrel!	*Auch ein Eichhörnchen!*	*OWKH ein EIKH-huhrn-khen!*

◉ SIGHTSEEING

I'm glad you've installed gravel paths, handrails, garbage cans, benches and signposts every 100 meters.	*Ich bin so froh, daß Sie für all die Kieswege, Geländer, Abfalleimer, Bänke und alle 100 Meter Wegweiser gesorgt haben.*	*Eekh bin zoh FROH, dahss zee fewr AHLL dee KEES-vay-geh, Geh-LEN-dair, AHP-fahll-EI-mair, BAIN-keh oont AHL-leh HOON-dairt MAY-tair VAIG-vei-zair geh-ZORKT hah-ben.*
Nevertheless, we are lost.	*Trotzdem haben wir uns verlaufen.*	*TROHTS-daim hah-ben veer oons fair-LOW-fen.*
Could you direct us to the parking lot?	*Könnten Sie uns den Weg zum Parkplatz zeigen?*	*KUHN-ten zee OONS dain VAIG tsoom PAHRK-plahts TSEI-gen?*

HOW TO PICK UP A RHEIN MAIDEN

Skiing single is a superb way for guys to meet tanned, limber German women. Once a *Meinhoffer* (dude) is on a chair lift with one, she is immobilized and subject to his clever repartee.

I saw you on the slope.	*Ich sah Sie auf der Piste.*	*Eekh ZAH zee owf dair PEE-steh.*
What beautiful form you have!	*Was für eine tolle Form Sie haben!*	*VAHS fewr ei-neh TOHL-leh FOHRM zee HAH-ben!*
Your skiing is good, too.	*Sie laufen auch gut Schi.*	*Zee LOW-fen owkh goot SHEE.*
Do you like my skis?	*Gefallen Ihnen meine Schier?*	*Geh-FAHL-len EE-nen mei-neh SHEE-air?*
They are long, yes?	*Sie sind lang, nicht wahr?*	*Zee zint LAHNG, neekht VAHR?*
Are you aware that ski length corresponds to strength and courage?	*Wußten Sie, daß Schilänge mit Kraft und Mut einhergeht?*	*VOOSS-ten zee, DAHSS SHEE-lehng-eh mit KRAHFT oont MOOT EIN-hair-GAIT?*
Say, do you like fondue/massage?	*Sagen Sie, mögen Sie Fondue/eine Massage?*	*ZAH-gen zee, MUH-gen zee fohn-DEW/ei-neh mah-SAH-sheh?*

MAN OR SUPERMAN

Many women like the blond
hair, athletic build
and haughty demeanor
of German men. Crack
their arrogance with
a few carefully chosen
phrases.

Excuse me, do you know a strong/experienced man who could help me?	*Entschuldigen Sie, kennen Sie einen starken/erfahrenen Mann, der mir helfen könnte?*	*Ent-SHOOL-dee-gen zee, KEN-nen zee ei-nen SHTAR-ken/air-FAH-ren-en MAHN, dair meer HELL-fen KUHN-teh?*
I'm having trouble with my car.	*Ich habe Probleme mit meinem Wagen.*	*Eekh HAH-beh proh-BLAY-meh mit MEI-nem VAH-gen.*
Perhaps I need a fresh set of plugs.	*Vielleicht brauche ich neue Zündkerzen.*	*Feel-LEIKHT BROW-kheh eekh NOY-eh TSUHNT-kair-tsen.*
Whom could I trust to handle a job like that?	*Wem könnte ich diesen Job anvertrauen?*	*VAIM kuhn-teh eekh dee-zen JOHB AHN-fair-TROW-en?*
When shall I swing by?	*Wann soll ich vorbeikommen?*	*VAHN ZOLL eekh fohr-BEI-kohm-men?*

ANARCHY RULES

Discos are great places to meet anarchists, artists and vegetarians. Fashion is an important part of making friends with these people, so be sure to wear the right clothing and to admire that of your quarry.

I love your black boots/pants/shirt/jacket/hat/lipstick.	*Ich finde Deine Stiefel/Deine Hose/Dein Hemd/ Deine Jacke/ Deinen Hut/Deinen Lippenstift einfach toll. Alles in Schwarz.*	*Eekh FIN-deh dei-neh SHTEE-fell/ dei-neh HOH-zeh/ dein HEMT/dei-neh YAHK-keh/dei-nen HOOT/dei-nen LEEP-pen-SHTEEFT EIN-fahkh TOHLL. AHL-less in SHVARTS.*
Do you also like my black boots/pants/shirt/jacket/hat/lipstick?	*Finden Sie meine schwarzen Stiefel/ meine Hose/mein Hemd/meine Jacke/meinen Hut/ meinen Lippenstift auch gut?*	*Fin-den zee MEI-neh SHVAHR-tsen SHTEE-fell/ HOH-zeh/HEMT/ YAHK-keh/ HOOT/ LEEP-pen-SHTEEFT OWKH goot?*
I could see right away you're an alternative person.	*Ich habe gleich bemerkt—du bist ein Alternativer.*	*Eekh HAH-beh GLEIKH beh-MAIRKT—doo bist ein ahl-TAIR-nah-TEE-fair.*

No one could wear more black than you do.	*Keiner könnte mehr Schwarz tragen also du.*	*KEI-nair KUHN-teh mair SHVAHRTS trah-gen ahls DOO.*
Let me pay with money from my black wallet and we'll leave on my black bicycle.	*Laß mich mit Geld aus meinem schwarzen Portemonnaie zahlen, und wir nehmen dann mein schwarzes Fahrrad.*	*LAHSS meekh mit GELT ows mei-nem SHVAR-tsen POHRT-moh-nay TSAH-len, oont veer NAY-men dahn mein SHVAR-tses FAHR-raht.*
What? You're holding out for a black Mercedes?	*Was? Du bestehst auf einem schwarzen Mercedes?*	*VAHS? Doo beh-SHTAYST owf ein-nem SHVAR-tsen mair-SAY-dess?*

THE WORDS OF LOVE AND PASTRY

Germans feel such a deep passion for pastry that they use the same phrases with their bakers and lovers. Use these examples to get the dessert you want.

What lovely honey cakes/sugar tarts you have.	*Sie haben so schönen Honigkuchen/so schöne Zuckertorte.*	*Zee HAH-ben zoh SHUH-nen HOH-neekh-KOO-khen/ zoh SHUH-neh TSOOK-air-TOHR-teh.*
I can't sleep at night thinking of your muffin/ marmalade.	*Ich kann in der Nacht nicht schla-fen, da ich an Ihre Küchlein/ Marmelade denke.*	*Eekh KAHN in dair NAHKHT NEEKHT SHLAH-fen, dah eekh ahn EE-reh KUHKH-lein/ mahr-meh-LAH-deh DAIN-keh.*
Give me your finest sticky buns/ Bavarian cream.	*Geben Sie mir Ihre feinsten klebrig-süßen Brötchen/ Ihre feinste bay-erische Sahne.*	*GAY-ben zee meer EE-reh FEIN-sten KLAY-breekh-ZEWS-sen BRUHT-khen/EE-reh FEIN-steh bei-AIR-ree-sheh ZAH-neh.*

I want to bite your bundt cake.	*Ich möchte in Ihren Gugelhupf beißen.*	*Eekh MUHKH-teh in EE-ren GOO-gel-hoopf BEIS-sen.*
You're killing me.	*Sie bringen mich um.*	*Zee BREEN(G)-en meekh OOM.*
I adore you.	*Ich bete Sie an.*	*Eekh BAY-teh zee AHN.*
Same time tomorrow?	*Morgen zur gleichen Zeit?*	*MOHR-gen tsoor GLEI-khen TSEIT?*

MIX & MATCH MUSICAL COMMENTARY

Germans believe every civilized person should be able to discuss music in German. When the subject comes up—and it will—show how refined you are by choosing one phrase from each of these columns to create a genuine-sounding comment.

SENTIMENT	ARTIST	ADJECTIVE	NOUN
I long for	**Beethoven's**	**sickeningly beautiful**	**bassoon parts.**
Ich sehne mich nach	*Beethovens*	*schrecklich schönen*	*Fagottparts.*
Eekh ZAY-neh meekh nahkh	*BAY-toh-fens*	*Shrek-leekh SHUH-nen*	*fah-GOHT-pahrts.*
I could almost touch	**Mozart's**	**velvety**	**adagio.**
Ich könnte fast berühren	*Mozarts*	*samtenes*	*Adagio.*
Eekh KUHN-teh fahst beh-RYOO-ren	*Moht-tsarts*	*zahm-teh-ness*	*Ah-DAH-jee-oh.*

SENTIMENT	ARTIST	ADJECTIVE	NOUN
I admire	**Wagner's**	**enormous**	**Henrietta.**
Ich bewundere	*Wagners*	*enorme*	*Henrietta.*
Eekh beh VOON-deh-reh	*VAHG-nairs*	*ay-NOHR-meh*	*Hen-ree-AY-teh.*
I bathe my psychic wounds in	**Handel's**	**scanty**	**G chords.**
Ich bade meine Wunden in	*Händels*	*knappen*	*G-Akkorden.*
Eekh BAH-deh mei-neh VOON-den in	*HEN-dells*	*KNAHP-pen*	*GAY-ahk-KOHR-den.*
I was moved by	**Schubert's**	**pulsing bronze**	**princess.**
Ich war gerührt von	*Schuberts*	*impulsiver, braungebrannter*	*Prinzessin.*
Eekh vahr geh-REWRT fohn	*SHOO-bairts*	*EEM-pool-ZEE-vair, BROWN-geh-BRAHN-tair*	*preen-TSES-seen.*

THE GALLANT DUELIST

The centuries-old tradition of dueling is dying out in German universities, even in Heidelberg. Swordplay is rarely a part of romantic rivalry today, but physical confrontation can still occur. Use these phrases to avoid personal injury.

She means nothing to me.	*Sie bedeutet mir nichts.*	*Zee beh-DOY-tet meer NEEKHTS.*
I regret ever meeting/kissing/fondling/marrying her.	*Ich bedauere, sie je getroffen/geküßt/gestreichelt/geheiratet zu haben.*	*Eekh beh-DOW-air-eh, zee YAY geh-TROHF-fen/ge-KUHST/geh-SHTREI-khelt/ge-HEI-rah-tet tsoo HAH-ben.*
Yes, I would be happy to cut off your nose at dawn.	*Ja, ich würde dir gerne in der Dämmerung die Nase abschneiden.*	*YAH, eekh VEWR-deh deer GAIR-neh in dair DEM-mair-oon(g) dee NAH-zeh AHB-schnei-den.*
Unfortunately, my plane leaves in 15 minutes.	*Leider fliegt mein Flugzeug in 15 Minuten ab.*	*LEI-dair fleekt mein FLOOK-tsoykh in FUHNF-tsain mee-NOO-ten AHP.*
She's all yours.	*Sie ist ganz die deine.*	*Zee ist GAHNTS dee DEI-neh.*

ESCAPE FROM OOMPAH

Oompah is central to German culture. To avoid spending precious vacation time listening to it, use a combination of realistic-sounding excuses and manipulation.

What a pity. I cannot attend.	*Schade. Ich kahn nicht dabeisein.*	*SHAH-deh. EEKH kahn NEEKHT dah-BEI-zein.*
The sound of an accordion gives me hives/seizures.	*Tut mir leid, aber ich kriege Pickel/Anfälle von Akkordeontönen.*	*TOOT meer LEIT, ah-bair eekh KREE-geh PEEK-kell/AHN-fell-eh fohn ahk-KOHR-day-ohn-TUH-nen.*
I'll spend the evening alone.	*Ich verbringe den Abend allein.*	*Eekh fair-BREEN(G)-eh dain AH-bent ah-LEIN.*
There's a documentary tonight about German regional costumes/cheeses!	*Und es gibt im fernsehen einen Dokumentarfilm über deutsche Trachten/Käse!*	*Oont es GEEPT im FAIRN-zay-en ei-nen DOH-KOO-men-TAHR-feelm ew-bair DOY-cheh TRAHKH-ten/KAY-zeh!*
Could I borrow your Porsche while you're out?	*Darf ich deinen Porsche borgen, während du weg bist?*	*Dahrf eekh DEI-nen POR-sheh bohr-gen, vair-ent doo VAIK bist?*

SURVIVING GERMAN ROMANTICISM

A visitor who becomes intimate with a lonely *Hausfrau* or traveling salesman may need these phrases to deal with big issues in a sensitive, diplomatic way.

My darling, I've never slept with such a robust person before.	*Mein Schatz, ich habe bisher noch nie mit so einem solchen Kraftprotz geschlafen.*	*Mein SHAHTS, eekh HAH-beh BEESS-hair nohkh NEE mit ZOH ei-nem KRAHFT-prohts geh-SHLAH-fen.*
I fear you will roll over and crush me like a Moselle grape.	*Ich fürchte, du wirst dich umdrehen und mich zerquetschen wie eine Moseltraube zerquetschen.*	*Eekh FEWRKH-teh, doo VEERST deekh oom-DRAY-en oont MEEKH vee EI-neh MOH-zell-TROW-bee tsair-KVET-shen.*
Your breath/gas smells like sauerkraut from hell.	*Dein Atem/ Gepfurze riecht wie höllisches Sauerkraut.*	*Dein AH-tem/ geh-PFOOR-tseh reekht vee HUHL-lee-shess ZOW-air-krowt.*
If you don't mind, my pumpkin, I'll sleep on the sofa.	*Wenn Du nichts dagegen hast, mein Kürbis, schlafe ich auf dem Sofa.*	*Venn doo NEEKHTS dah-GAY-gen hast, mein KER-biss, SHLAH-feh eekh owf daim ZOH-fah.*

MAGIC MOUNTAIN OF MARKS

To do business in Germany you must follow German protocol. That means razor-sharp promptness, complete titles and groveling.

Although almost all the business people you meet will speak English and hold doctorates, they will appreciate your crude attempts to flatter them in their native tongue.

The very honorable mister doctor Klodhopper.	*Sehr verehrter Herr Doktor Klodhopper.*	*Zair fair-AIR-ter hair OOHK-tohr Klodhopper.*
We need more of those fine products of yours, mister esteemed doktor, sir.	*Wir benötigen mehr Ihrer hervorragenden Produkte, werter Herr Doktor.*	*Veer beh-NUH-tee-gen MAIR EE-rair hair-fohr-RAH-gen-den proh-DOOK-teh, vair-ter hair DOHK-tohr.*
When our customers see the words "MADE IN GERMANY," they whip out their credit cards without another thought.	*Wenn unsere Kunden die Worte "MADE IN GERMANY" sehen, zücken sie ihre Kreditkarten, ohne nachzudenken.*	*Venn OON-zair-eh KOON-den dee VOHR-teh "MADE IN GERMANY" ZAY-en, TSUHK-ken zee ee-reh KRAY-deet-KAHR-ten, oh-neh NAHKH-tsoo-dain-ken.*

BUSINESS 💼

We are short in the mark department, however.	*Wir sind allerdings, was die Mark anbelangt, knapp bei Kasse.*	*VEER zint AHL-lair-din(g)z, vahs dee MAHRK AHN-be-lahnkt, KNAHP bei KAHS-seh.*
Would you consider taking an out-of-continent promissory note?	*Würden Sie eventuell einen nicht kontinentalen Schuldschein akzeptieren?*	*VEWR-den zee ay-ven-too-ELL ei-nen NEEKHT kohn-tee-nen-TAHL-en SHOOLT-shein ahk-tsep-TEE-ren?*

PROMPTNESS HINTS

Politeness requires that you break the plane of the building entrance at the appointed hour; therefore you are expected either to ring the bell or knock four seconds before the agreed appointment time. Other hints are:

• When making a date with anyone synchronize watches to the nearest 100th of a second.

• When calculating travel time, consider drag coefficients, wind direction and speed, and body fat.

AUTOGESPRÄCHE

As every red-blooded German businessman loves cars, the subject makes good business small talk. Use these questions to pave the way with your hosts.

Who makes the most intimidating cars: BMW, Mercedes or Porsche?	*Wer macht die einschüchternsten Autos: BMW, Mercedes oder Porsche?*	*VAIR mahkt dee ein-SHUHKH-tairn-sten OW-tohs? BAY-EM-VAY, mair-KAY-dess oh-dair POHR-sheh?*
Which will be the first to break the sound barrier?	*Welches wird als erstes die Schallmauer durchbrechen?*	*VEL-khess veerd ahls AIR-stess dee SHAHLL-mow-air DOORKH-brekh-en?*
Are any of them able to clear a path through bumper-to-bumper traffic?	*Sind irgendwelche davon in der Lage, sich im Stau klare Bahn zu verschaffen?*	*Zint EER-gent vell-kheh da-FOHN in dair LAH-geh, seekh im SHTOW KLAR-eh BAHN zu fair-SHAHF-fen?*
Do you agree that air-to-air missiles should be standard equipment?	*Meinen Sie, daß Luft-Luft-Raketen zur Standard-ausrüstung ge-hören sollten?*	*Mei-nen zee, dahss LOOFT-looft-rah-KAY-ten tsoor SHTAHN-dart-OWS-REWS-toon(g) geh-HUH-ren ZOHLL-ten?*

THE INEVITABLE THANK-YOU NOTE

Experienced travelers write prompt thank-you notes to hosts and hostesses. They are thus invited to return and may avoid troubles like irksome hotel and restaurant bills. It's not a bad idea to remind your benefactors of your value as a friend, as in this typical letter.

Dear Miss/Mrs./Mister Doktor,	*Sehr geehrte Frau/Sehr geehrter Herr Doktor.*
Our little drive was thrilling.	*Unsere kleine Fahrt war aufregend.*
Your car is like a missile.	*Ihr Wagen ist wie eine Rakete.*
Now I have terrible nightmares.	*Nun habe ich schreckliche Alpträume.*
Don't worry that you were overtaken on the *Autobahn.*	*Machen Sie sich nichts daraus, daß Sie auf der Autobahn überholt wurden.*
It could happen to anyone.	*Das kann jedem passieren.*
It will be our secret.	*Es bleibt unser Geheimnis.*
Thanks again,	*Nochmals vielen Dank,*